My Science Library

Stop And Go, Fast And Slow:

Moving Objects in Different Ways

by Buffy Silverman

Science Content Edi~~~~
Kristi Lew

ROURKE CLASSROOM

www.rourkeclassroom.com

Science content editor: Kristi Lew

A former high school teacher with a background in biochemistry and more than 10 years of experience in cytogenetic laboratories, Kristi Lew specializes in taking complex scientific information and making it fun and interesting for scientists and non-scientists alike. She is the author of more than 20 science books for children and teachers.

© 2012 Rourke Publishing LLC

www.rourkeclassroom.com

Photo credits: Cover © 3dart, Cover logo frog © Eric Pohl, test tube © Sergey Lazarev; Page 3 © Zurijeta; Page 5 © Andrew Lundquist; Page 7 © Jane September; Page 9 © Jane September; Page 11 © nikkytok; Page 13 © Blue Door Publishing; Page 15 © Blue Door Publishing; Page 17 © Furchin
Page 19 © Nick Stubbs; Page 20 © James Blinn; Page 22 © Andrew Lundquist, Jane September, Blue Door Publishing
Page 23 © Furchin, nikkytok, Blue Door Publishing

Editor: Kelli Hicks

My Science Library series produced for Rourke by Blue Door Publishing, Florida

Library of Congress Cataloging-in-Publication Data

Silverman, Buffy.
 Stop and go, fast and slow : moving objects in different ways / Buffy Silverman.
    p. cm. -- (My science library)
 ISBN 978-1-61741-727-6 (Hard cover)
 ISBN 978-1-61741-929-4 (Soft cover)
 1. Force and energy--Juvenile literature. I. Title.
 QC73.4.S545 2012
 531'.113--dc22
                              2011003864

Rourke Publishing
Printed in China, Voion Industry
 Guangdong Province
042011
042011LP

www.rourkeclassroom.com - rourke@rourkepublishing.com
Post Office Box 643328 Vero Beach, Florida 32964

You make things move with a **push** or **pull**. Push a toy car. The car zooms.

Pull a wagon. It rolls to the park.

Push a swing hard. Your energy makes the swing go high.

Push it soft. Your energy makes it swing low.

Push a bowling ball. It rolls away in a **straight** line.

Pull up marbles. They **zigzag** down.

Push on a **seesaw**. You go up high. Your friend goes down low.

Push a merry-go-round. It turns around and around. It **spins** fast.

A merry-go-round slows.
Then it stops.

What else can you move?

1. Can you name two ways to make things move?

2. When one side of a seesaw goes up. What happens to the other side?

3. How does a merry-go-round move?

Picture Glossary

pull (PUL):
To pull is to move something towards you.

push (PUSH):
To push is to move something away from you by pressing against it.

seesaw (SEE-saw):
A seesaw is a long board that goes up and down. A person sits on each end of the board.

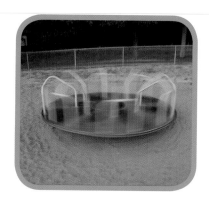

spins (SPINZ):
To spin is to turn quickly around and around.

straight (STRAYT):
Something that moves straight goes in one direction without turning.

zigzag (ZIG-zag):
Something that moves zigzag makes short, sharp turns.

Index

Websites

http://www.bbc.co.uk/schools/scienceclips/ages/5_6/
    pushes_pulls_fs.shtml

http://www.bbc.co.uk/schools/ks2bitesize/science/
    physical_processes/forces_action/play.shtml

http://pbskids.org/curiousgeorge/games/pogo_gogo/
    pogo_gogo.html

About the Author

Buffy Silverman looks up, down, and all around for animals and wildflowers. She writes about nature and science from her home in Michigan.